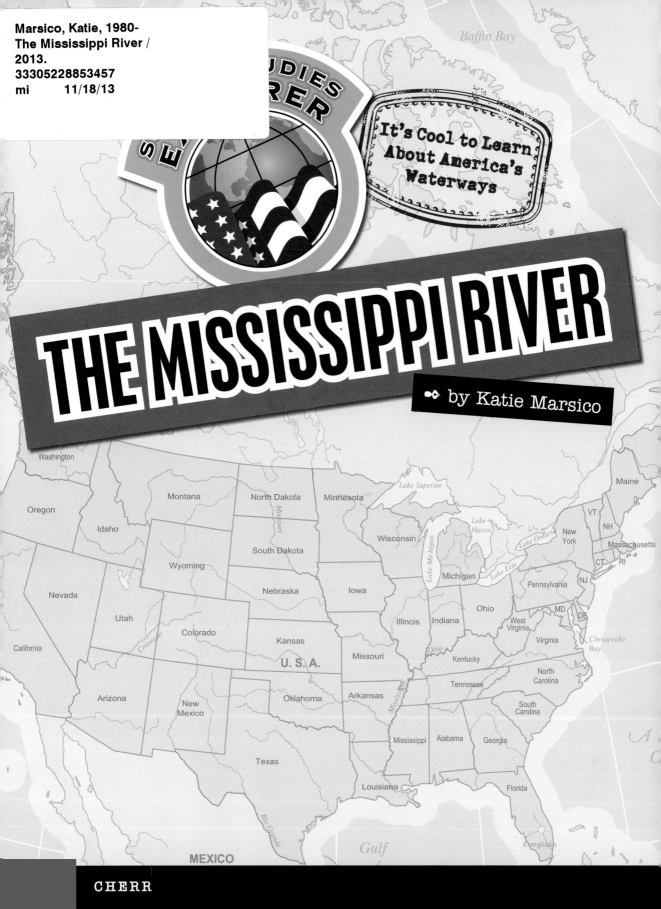

It's Cool to Learn About America's Waterways

THE MISSISSIPPI RIVER

➻ by Katie Marsico

Published in the United States of America
by Cherry Lake Publishing
Ann Arbor, Michigan
www.cherrylakepublishing.com

Content Adviser: James Wolfinger, PhD, Associate Professor,
History and Teacher Education, DePaul University, Chicago, Illinois

Book Design: The Design Lab

Photo Credits: Cover and page 3, ©J. McCormick/Shutterstock, Inc.,
©Robynrg/Shutterstock, Inc., ©iStockphoto.com/DenisTangneyJr, ©Kiev.
Victor/Shutterstock, Inc.; cover and page 4, ©Tony Campbell/Shutterstock,
Inc.; back cover and page 3, ©spirit of america/Shutterstock, Inc.; page
5, ©Imagestate Media Partners Limited - Impact Photos/Alamy; page 6,
©Nancy Bauer/Shutterstock, Inc.; page 8, ©fotokik_dot_com/Shutterstock,
Inc.; page 9, ©Nathan Benn/Alamy; page 10, ©Paul Orr/Shutterstock,
Inc.; page 11, ©July Flower/Shutterstock, Inc.; page 12, ©Aliaksandr
Nikitsin/Dreamstime.com; page 13, ©PVstock.com/Alamy; page 14,
©Andreas Nilsson/Shutterstock, Inc.; page 16, ©Rolf Nussbaumer
Photograph/Alamy; page 18, ©\North Wind Picture Archives/Alamy;
page 19, ©iofoto/Shutterstock, Inc.; page 20, ©Dana Ward/Shutterstock,
Inc.; page 23, ©bonchan/Shutterstock, Inc.; page 26, ©3841128876/
Shutterstock, Inc.; page 28, ©Al Mueller/Shutterstock, Inc.

Library of Congress Cataloging-in-Publication Data
Marsico, Katie, 1980–
  The Mississippi River / by Katie Marsico.
       p. cm. — (It's cool to learn about America's waterways)
  Includes index.
  ISBN 978-1-62431-011-9 (lib. bdg.) — ISBN 978-1-62431-035-5 (pbk.)—
ISBN 978-1-62431-059-1 (e-book)
1. Mississippi River—Juvenile literature. I. Title.
  F351.M34 2013
  977—dc23   2012037581

Cherry Lake Publishing would like to acknowledge the work
of The Partnership for 21st Century Skills. Please visit
www.21stcenturyskills.org for more information.

Printed in the United States of America
Corporate Graphics Inc.
January 2013
CLSP12

THE MISSISSIPPI RIVER

TABLE OF CONTENTS

LOUISIANA

CHAPTER ONE

WELCOME TO THE MISSISSIPPI RIVER!

➼ You might catch a glimpse of a bald eagle perched along the banks of the Mississippi River.

Get ready for an exciting adventure along a famous American waterway—the Mississippi River! Many people say the Mississippi is the most important river in the United States. It is the third-longest river in North America. It is also a major shipping route between the Midwest and the Gulf of Mexico. The Mississippi is a source of everything from drinking water to fun **recreational** activities. As you explore the Mississippi, you'll see a wide variety of wildlife, including river otters and bald eagles. In addition, you'll catch a glimpse of

a 19th-century fort and the tallest man-made monument in the country. You'll even have an opportunity to sample fresh catfish and a popular local dessert known as mud pie. Finally, you'll learn what you can do to help protect the mighty Mississippi River.

Before you start packing, though, you need to know exactly where you're headed. The Mississippi River begins at Lake Itasca in northwestern Minnesota. It then flows south all the way to the Gulf of Mexico in southeastern Louisiana. Its total length is about 2,500 miles (4,023.4 kilometers).

Whenever you explore a river, you might want to check out the area known as its delta. This low-lying, triangular-shaped strip of land is made up of soil, sand, clay, and gravel that are carried by the river's flowing water. Most deltas form where a river empties into the sea. The Mississippi River delta in Louisiana includes 3 million acres (1.2 million hectares) of coastal wetlands as well as some of the most fertile soil in the world.

The Mississippi River winds through Minnesota, Wisconsin, Iowa, Illinois, Missouri, Kentucky, Tennessee, Arkansas, Mississippi, and Louisiana. In all, you'll need to explore parts of 31 states and two Canadian provinces to fully tour its watershed, or basin. This is the region drained by the river and all its **tributaries**. Two major tributaries that flow into the Mississippi are the Ohio and Missouri Rivers. Other tributaries include the Saint Croix, Wisconsin, Rock, Illinois, Kaskaskia, Minnesota, Des Moines, White, Arkansas, and Red Rivers.

The Mississippi River's watershed is the fourth-largest in the world. It covers 1.2 million square miles (3.1 million sq km). This area reaches from the Allegheny Mountains in the east to the Rocky Mountains in the west. It even includes portions of southern Canada! (For your first adventure, however, you should probably stick to the section that is located in the United States.)

•◆ The Mississippi River forms the border between Wisconsin and Iowa.

MAPPING THE MISSISSIPPI RIVER

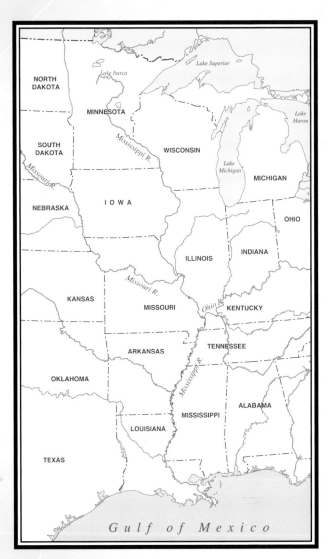

Take some time to review this map of the Mississippi River. Then lay a separate piece of paper over it. Trace over the waterway. Show where Lake Itasca and the Gulf of Mexico are located. Also mark where the Ohio and Missouri Rivers flow. Finally, label Minnesota, Wisconsin, Iowa, Illinois, Missouri, Kentucky, Tennessee, Arkansas, Mississippi, and Louisiana. Add any other important sites you learn about as you continue exploring the Mississippi River!

STOP
Don't write in this book!

→ The Mississippi River begins in Minnesota, running south through cities such as Minneapolis.

You might be wondering how you should pack for a journey along the Mississippi. For starters, don't assume that the only piece of clothing you'll need is a swimsuit! It's true that you'll be exploring a river. Yet that doesn't mean you're going to spend all your time in the water. The Mississippi supports a huge basin that features many kinds of amazing **habitats**.

You'll get a better picture of the river's **ecosystem** if you use your imagination. Think of the watershed as split into two separate regions. One region is the Upper Mississippi. People often describe this as the portion of the basin between northwestern Minnesota and southern Illinois. This area contains many freshwater lakes and deep river valleys. In addition, you'll probably notice prairie potholes. These shallow,

sunken marshes were created by the movement of **glaciers** thousands of years ago. The Upper Mississippi also has tallgrass prairies and mixed forests that include a combination of deciduous trees—which shed their leaves every year— and evergreens.

Once you move south of where the Ohio River joins the Mississippi in southern Illinois, you'll be in the second region, known as the Lower Mississippi. During your tour of this region, be prepared to slosh through swamps, marshes, and **bottomland forests**. The Lower Mississippi was once filled with these natural habitats, but the local ecosystem has slowly changed. People have cleared a large number of wetlands along the Mississippi River to make room for farms and cities.

•• The Mississippi and Ohio Rivers meet in Cairo, Illinois.

The Mississippi River itself features a variety of conditions. Some parts of the waterway are less than 3 feet (0.9 meters) deep. Others have depths of about 200 feet (61 m). Water temperature depends on which portion of the river you are touring and what time of year you are visiting. In summer, the Mississippi has gotten as warm as 88 degrees Fahrenheit (31.1 degrees Celsius) close to where it flows into the Gulf of Mexico. Farther north, however, parts of the river sometimes freeze over during colder months.

As you pack your suitcase, think about local climate, as well. If you're traveling across the Upper Mississippi region

•• Water temperatures in the Mississippi tend to drop during cooler autumn months.

→ During winter, many parts of the Mississippi River are sometimes covered in ice.

from December through February, pack thick sweaters. From June through August, however, shorts and T-shirts will do the trick! Weather in this region includes cold, snowy winters and hot summers. Not as much rain falls here as in the Lower Mississippi, which has a more humid climate. Winter weather in the lower portion of the basin is generally less extreme than in the upper section.

No matter where you're headed along the Mississippi, be aware of the potential for serious weather problems. **Droughts** and bad flooding sometimes occur in the watershed. But rather than worry about the weather, simply play it safe and check out the local forecast before you leave!

CHAPTER TWO

THE WATERWAY'S WILDLIFE

➼ A variety of deciduous trees along the banks of the Mississippi change color in the fall.

You'll need to pack more than clothes if you want to do some serious wildlife watching along the Mississippi River. For instance, it's a good idea to take along a camera. Plan on taking photos of the several types of trees that fill the forests of the Upper Mississippi. Willows, elms, sycamores, maples, oaks, walnuts, spruces, and pines all grow throughout this region. You'll also discover grasslike plants called sedges sprouting near the upper portion of the river.

As you explore this area, you'll likely spot colorful water lilies and lotuses floating in the Mississippi. If you're lucky, you might even spy the blue petals of the northern monkshood. This buttercup grows in the Upper Mississippi but is threatened. In other words, there's a good chance it will eventually face the risk of being wiped off the planet.

White, red, and black oaks rise up from the Lower Mississippi. Bitternut and shagbark hickories grow there, too. So do tulip trees, American elms, sassafrases, shortleaf pines, and eastern red cedars. You'll also run across a tall prairie grass known as bluestem, along with woody vines, mosses, and ferns.

◦◦ The Mississippi serves as a habitat for water plants such as the lotus.

Bring along a pair of binoculars, too. Then you can get a good look at the hundreds of birds that soar over the river's watershed. The Upper Mississippi is home to a large number of nesting bald eagles. You might also notice great egrets, red-tailed hawks, Canada geese, turkey vultures, and several kinds of swallows.

As you peer through your binoculars, keep your eyes peeled for mammals. Look for river otters, deer, bobcats, coyotes, and black bears. The Upper Mississippi also features many different types of reptiles and **amphibians**. These include snapping turtles, timber rattlesnakes, and bullfrogs. Alligator gar,

➺ Despite its name, the crayfish is not actually a fish. It is related to shrimps, crabs, and lobsters.

Much of the Mississippi River is made up of freshwater habitats. Closer to where the river empties into the Gulf of Mexico, the water becomes brackish. This is a combination of freshwater and saltwater. Some species, including bull sharks, are able to survive in freshwater, brackish water, and saltwater. Bull sharks in the Mississippi River have been found not only near the gulf but as far north as Illinois!

northern pike, silver lampreys, and pugnose shiners make up much of the local fish population. **Mussels** and tiny lobsterlike animals called crayfish are also found in the Upper Mississippi.

You'll observe several of these same underwater creatures in the Lower Mississippi. There are also fish such as sturgeons, bowfins, catfish, and darters. Always be aware of your surroundings as you study animals in this portion of the river. Otherwise, you might be surprised when an American alligator sneaks up on you!

●◆ The red-cockaded woodpecker is in danger of dying out.

The Lower Mississippi serves as a habitat for a variety of reptiles and amphibians, including glass lizards, copperhead snakes, and dusky **salamanders**. Local mammals range from gray squirrels and cottontail rabbits to nine-banded armadillos and Florida panthers. When you search for birds in the Lower Mississippi, you'll probably see blue jays, warblers, and tanagers. Be sure to listen as you look at the woods and wetlands around you. If you hear a tapping noise, it might be a red-cockaded woodpecker! Sadly, this species is endangered. That means it faces an immediate and serious threat to its survival.

Now it's time to close up your suitcase and start heading toward the river. Be prepared for a few fun history lessons along the way!

Make Your Very Own Field Guide

Is your head spinning after reading about all of the plants and animals that are part of the Mississippi River's ecosystem? If so, it will be easier to stay organized with a field guide. This is a book that describes the different species found within a certain environment. There's no need to buy a field guide for the Mississippi River. You can make your own! First, pick 20 local species (or more if you want). Write the name of each one on a separate sheet of paper. Then get ready to do some detective work on the computer or at the library. Track down and record the following information for the plants and animals you have selected:

Type of plant/animal: (tree, shrub,
    flower/reptile, mammal, or fish)
Habitat:
Appearance:
Other interesting facts:

When you're finished, either print out or sketch pictures of the species in your field guide. Finally, decorate a cover and staple your pages together. Or you can snap them into a binder. Remember to pack your field guide before you leave for your adventure along the Mississippi River!

CHAPTER THREE

PAST AND PRESENT

➥ The Sioux are among the many American Indian groups who lived in the area around the Mississippi River.

As you get closer to the Mississippi River, picture yourself arriving in the area roughly 12,000 years ago. This is when huge lakes formed by melting glaciers overflowed into what is now the Mississippi River valley. The result was the creation of the waterway you're about to explore!

Not long after, early peoples began hunting throughout the Mississippi basin. During the next several thousand years, many American Indian groups developed farms and villages there. They included the Cheyenne, Sioux, Ojibwe, Potawatomi, Kickapoo, Tamaroa, and Chickasaw.

Europeans began exploring the Mississippi River in the 16th century. Until the early 1800s, countries such as France, Spain, and Great Britain claimed parts of the basin. By 1815, however, various agreements reached with these nations gave the United States control of the waterway.

Since then, the Mississippi has shaped a huge part of the culture and **economy** of the United States. People rely on the river to ship goods from farms and factories in the Midwest to ports along the Gulf of Mexico. In addition, about 92 percent of the farm products that Americans sell to other countries come from the Mississippi's watershed. These items include corn, soybeans, wheat, cotton, rice, cattle, and hogs.

•❖ Goods are shipped up and down the Mississippi on large boats called barges.

More than 72 million people live in the Mississippi River's watershed. Minneapolis–Saint Paul, Minnesota; Saint Louis, Missouri; and New Orleans, Louisiana, are major cities on the river.

Think about kicking off your travels with a little outdoor adventure. Visit the Mississippi National River and Recreation Area in Minnesota. This is the perfect place to begin your journey if you want to hike, bike, boat, camp, or watch wildlife. The park stretches for 72 miles (115.9 km) along the waterway. If you'd prefer to find out more about the region's history, check out Minnesota's historic Fort Snelling. The fort dates back to the early 1820s. It features exhibits on everything from local American Indians to 19th-century fur traders.

• Music clubs are among the attractions for visitors to New Orleans.

ACTIVITY

TEST YOUR KNOWLEDGE

How well do you know the history of the Mississippi River? Find out by taking the quick quiz below! On the left side, you'll see the names of five people who are linked to the waterway. On the right side, you'll see a description of the various reasons these men and women are famous. Try to match each person with the correct description!

1) René-Robert Cavelier Sieur de La Salle

A) Former slave who used escape routes along the river to help Southern slaves flee to freedom in the North

2) Tecumseh

B) Writer who was known as Mark Twain and is famous for his novels about life along the Mississippi

3) Harriet Tubman

C) Shawnee leader who traveled throughout much of the Mississippi River valley in an effort to unite American Indian groups to fight ongoing white settlement

4) Samuel Clemens

D) Athlete who swam the length of the Mississippi River in 68 days

5) Martin Strel

E) European who claimed the Mississippi River basin for France during the late 1600s

Answers: 1) E; 2) C; 3) A; 4) B; 5) D

STOP
Don't write in this book!

When you tour Fort Snelling, you can find out more about the American Civil War (1861–1865). One of the main reasons this conflict occurred was because Northern and Southern states differed over the issue of slavery. Northern soldiers trained at Fort Snelling before facing Southern troops. Down the river, stop in Vicksburg, Mississippi, which was the site of a famous and bloody Civil War battle.

Be sure to leave time in your schedule for the Lower Mississippi, too. The Gateway Arch in Saint Louis, Missouri, offers a great view of the waterway—from 630 feet (192 m) above the ground! The arch is the tallest man-made monument in the United States.

Remember to also visit New Orleans, Louisiana. There you can book a Mississippi riverboat cruise. Try to relax while you're on the water, especially since you'll need some extra energy for dancing. The Lower Mississippi is a great location to tap your feet to country songs or enjoy the best of the blues.

Moving to the beat will probably make you work up an appetite. Don't forget to grab a bite to eat. You'll find many different **cuisines** throughout the Mississippi basin, and they're all

worth sampling! Barbecued ribs, fried chicken, and fresh cat-fish are tasty examples of dishes you'll encounter there.

The Lower Mississippi also features a variety of spicy Cajun foods such as jambalaya and gumbo. Cajun foods combine Southern and French cooking styles. Jambalaya is made from rice, tomatoes, peppers, onions, celery, and ham, sausage, chicken, or shellfish. Gumbo is a thick soup or stew prepared with either chicken or seafood and a vegetable called okra. Once you've finished eating, get ready to say good-bye to the Mississippi River. Before you leave, however, you need to learn about some serious issues affecting this incredible American waterway.

◆◆ Jambalaya is especially popular in the Mississippi River delta region.

After your action-packed adventure along the Mississippi River, you deserve a little dessert! Mississippi mud pie isn't made from real mud, of course. The dish got its name because its gooey chocolate filling reminds people of the river's muddy shores. There are a few different ways to prepare this tasty treat. The recipe below is simple—and even includes make-believe bugs slithering through your Mississippi mud!

Mississippi Mud Pie

INGREDIENTS

2 cups milk
1 package of instant chocolate pudding
12 chocolate sandwich cookies (such as Oreos)

Gummy worms
Whipped cream
Black sprinkles

INSTRUCTIONS

1. Add the milk to the instant pudding, and whisk the mixture with a spoon by stirring it with light, quick strokes.

2. Allow the pudding to set in your refrigerator for about 10 minutes. Meanwhile, place the chocolate sandwich cookies inside a plastic freezer bag. Close the bag and crush the cookies with a rolling pin. Then empty the crumbs into a pie tin and press them down lightly with your fingertips.

3. Next, take your chocolate pudding out of the refrigerator. Spoon roughly half of it into the pie tin and top your "Mississippi mud" with a handful of gummy worms.

4. Spread the rest of the pudding across the ingredients that are already in the pie tin. Then add more worms and a layer of whipped cream. Finally, coat your pie with black sprinkles (which are supposed to look like ants crawling across your mixture of "mud" and candy).

5. Dig in!!

CHAPTER FOUR

TAKING CARE OF A NATIONAL TREASURE

➻ Some factories along the Mississippi pollute the river.

The Mississippi River is famous for more than its amazing ecosystem and important role in the culture and economy of the United States. It is also known as America's second most-polluted waterway.

Chemicals from farms, factories, towns, and cities drain into the soil and eventually reach the Mississippi. In addition, people have cleared wetlands and forests to build farms and communities. As a result of this human activity, some animal species may vanish from the Mississippi River.

ACTIVITY

THE MISSISSIPPI RIVER

GRAPHING POLLUTED WATERWAYS

Scientists recently studied the top 10 U.S. waterways that suffer from toxic discharge, or poisonous chemicals that leak into the water. They discovered that more than 98 million pounds (44 million kilograms) of toxic discharge affected the 10 rivers and canals they focused on.

They noted that about 32 percent of these chemicals ended up in the Ohio River. Roughly 14 percent flowed into the New River. Approximately 13 percent polluted the Mississippi. The Savannah River was the fourth hardest-hit waterway, with about 8 percent of the discharge. A little more than 7 percent affected the Delaware River. The five remaining waterways in the study held about 26 percent of the poisonous chemicals among them.

Create a bar graph using the information you've just read. Can you guess which bar will be the longest? How do you think the bar for the Mississippi River will compare to the bars for the other waterways?

STOP Don't write in this book!

Percent of toxic discharge

40
30
20
10
0

Ohio River   New River   Mississippi River   Savannah River   Delaware River   Other rivers

The good news is that the Mississippi and its natural wonders don't have to disappear. Politicians, scientists, and people just like you are committed to supporting **conservation** in and along the river. One example of their efforts involves replanting trees in wetland forests that have been affected by pollution and development.

Sometimes conservation is as simple as sharing what you know. You can educate the public by talking to your friends and family about all that you have experienced during your Mississippi River adventure. Discuss the wildlife you've seen, as well as what you've learned about local culture and history. Tell everyone why the Mississippi is a remarkable American waterway. It should be respected, protected, and enjoyed for centuries to come.

◆ With your help, the mighty Mississippi will remain healthy and beautiful for many years to come.

Political leaders in the 31 states that form the Mississippi River's watershed have the power to make a big difference. Along with politicians across the rest of the nation, they vote on laws and create projects that impact America's waterways. Writing a letter to these men and women lets them know that people like you care about the Mississippi. Ask an adult to help you find the addresses of government officials who support conservation efforts. Then create a short, simple letter using the following outline:

Dear [INSERT THE NAME OF THE POLITICIAN(S) YOU DECIDE TO WRITE TO]:

I am writing to ask for your help in protecting the Mississippi River. The river is important to me because [INSERT TWO OR THREE REASONS THE RIVER MATTERS TO YOU].

Thanks for your efforts to support this amazing American waterway!

Sincerely,

[INSERT YOUR NAME]

STOP Don't write in this book!

GLOSSARY

amphibians (am-FIB-ee-uhnz) cold-blooded animals with a backbone that live in water and breathe with gills when young; as adults, they develop lungs and live on land

bottomland forests (BAH-tuhm-land FOR-ists) low-lying wetlands that feature wooded areas found along streams or rivers

conservation (kahn-sur-VAY-shuhn) the protection of valuable things, especially wildlife, natural resources, forests, or artistic or historic objects

cuisines (kwi-ZEENZ) styles or manners of cooking or presenting food

droughts (DROUTZ) long periods without rain

economy (i-KAH-nuh-mee) the system of buying, selling, making things, and managing money in a place

ecosystem (EE-koh-sis-tuhm) all the livings things in a place and their relation to the environment

glaciers (GLAY-shurz) slow-moving masses of ice found in mountain valleys or polar regions

habitats (HAB-uh-tats) places where an animal or a plant naturally lives

mussels (MUHS-uhlz) shellfish that have black shells and can be eaten

recreational (rek-ree-AY-shuhn-uhl) involving games, sports, and hobbies that people like to do in their spare time

salamanders (SAL-uh-man-durz) animals that look like small, brightly colored lizards

tributaries (TRIB-yu-ter-eez) streams that flow into a larger stream, river, or lake

FOR MORE INFORMATION

BOOKS

Johnson, Robin. *The Mississippi: America's Mighty River*. New York: Crabtree Publishing Company, 2010.

Tieck, Sarah. *Mark Twain*. Edina, MN: ABDO Publishing Company, 2010.

WEB SITES

National Park Service (NPS)—Mississippi National River and Recreation Area: For Kids
www.nps.gov/miss/forkids/index.htm
This Web site includes an online quiz and an art contest related to the Mississippi, along with information on becoming a junior ranger for the NPS.

The Nature Conservancy—The Mississippi River
www.nature.org/ourinitiatives/habitats/riverslakes/placesweprotect /mississippi-river.xml
This site features information about issues affecting the waterway, as well as what people are doing to save the Mississippi.

ABOUT THE AUTHOR
Katie Marsico has written more than 100 books for young readers. She was shocked to learn that bull sharks spend time in the Mississippi, but that won't stop her from further exploring the river!